Great Ideas of Science

THE BIG BANG

by Paul Fleisher

Twenty-First Century Books
Minneapolis

To Debra Sims Fleisher, with eternal appreciation for her support and love

The author would like to express appreciation to the following people for their assistance in the writing of this book: Michael Lemonick, for his image of a stretching rubber band as an analogy for the expanding universe in Echo of the Big Bang; *and Tom Sigfried for his especially clear description of the geometry of the universe in* Strange Matters.

The publisher wishes to thank Prof. Marco Peloso, cosmologist at the University of Minnesota–Twin Cities, for his assistance in the preparation of this book.

Twenty-First Century Books
A division of Lerner Publishing Group
241 First Avenue North
Minneapolis, Minnesota 55401 U.S.A.

Website address: www.lernerbooks.com

Library of Congress Cataloging-in-Publication Data

Fleisher, Paul
    The big bang / by Paul Fleisher.
      p.   cm. — (Great ideas of science)
    Includes bibliographical references and index.
    ISBN-13: 978–0–8225–2133–4 (lib. bdg. : alk. paper)
    ISBN-10: 0–8225–2133–4 (lib. bdg. : alk. paper)
    1. Big bang theory—Juvenile literature. 2. Cosmology—Juvenile literature. I. Title. III. Series.
    QB991.B54F53 2006
    523.1'8—dc22   2005001234

Manufactured in the United States of America
1 2 3 4 5 6 – BP – 11 10 09 08 07 06

TABLE of CONTENTS

INTRODUCTION

Look up into the starry sky. On a clear, dark night, it can seem like you're looking into a bottomless well. There are so many stars. Some are bright. Others are so faint you can barely see them. Where did they all come from?

People have always wondered about the origins of the universe. Early civilizations told myths (stories) to explain the creation of the cosmos. For example, according to one ancient Chinese myth, the universe began when a great creator-giant hatched from an egg. The world we know was made from the giant's body when he died. The ancient Greeks thought the gods created the universe out of chaos (infinite, formless space). Many cultures told stories of gods bringing forth the world from the waters or the sky. But as humans began to study the universe using the tools of science, they searched for explanations that matched their observations more closely.

The branch of science that studies the origin and structure of the universe is called cosmology.

Looking at a starry sky can make the universe seem endless.

Scientists who specialize in this field are called cosmologists. Until the early twentieth century, cosmology was little more than guesswork. Since then, new discoveries in physics and astronomy have turned cosmology into one of the liveliest fields of science. Over the past century, cosmologists have developed a detailed idea that describes the origin and evolution of our universe.

This is the story in a nutshell: The entire universe began in a single instant, in an unimaginably powerful explosion. That explosion created all time and space, all matter and energy. The cosmos has been expanding outward from that explosion for about fourteen billion years. The universe we see is what remains from that one fiery moment of creation.

This idea is known as the Big Bang theory. It is one of the most important theories of modern science. The Big Bang theory is not perfect or complete. It doesn't answer every question we have about the origin of the universe. Nevertheless, it is the best explanation we have of where the universe came from.

WHAT IS A THEORY?

When we try to explain something we don't understand, we make an educated guess. We might say, "I have a theory about that" and then give our explanation. Scientists call such an educated guess a hypothesis.

To a scientist, a theory is much more than a simple hypothesis. A theory is a *big* idea. A scientific theory gathers a broad group of facts and observations, and explains them all with one clear, simple idea. A theory must be supported by experimental evidence. And it should predict the results of observations scientists haven't yet made. It sets researchers on a quest to test the theory. They conduct new experiments to see if their measurements will support the theory or disprove it.

The Big Bang theory meets all of these requirements. It explains how the stars and planets formed. It explains why most of the matter in the universe is made of hydrogen and helium. It explains why the universe seems to be expanding in all directions. And most of all, it attempts to explain the origin of the universe itself.

CHAPTER 1

FINDING OUR PLACE IN THE UNIVERSE

Humans have always looked into the night sky and wondered about the mysteries hidden in its depths. Developing our modern understanding of the universe and its origins has taken thousands of years, with many wrong turns and detours along the way.

THE EARLY COSMOLOGISTS

Until the 1500s, most natural philosophers (the early scientists) thought our planet was the center of the universe. If Earth were moving through space, they reasoned, we would be thrown off or blown away by violent winds. In their theory, stars and planets circled Earth, held in a series of invisible crystal spheres. It certainly looked like the natural philosophers were right. After all, as we gaze up at the sky, don't we seem to be standing still? The Moon, the Sun, and the stars travel across the sky in great circles above us.

This geocentric (Earth-centered) theory survived for almost two thousand years. It was supported in the writings of the Greek philosopher Aristotle around 350 BCE. About five hundred years later, in the second century A.D., the Egyptian astronomer Ptolemy wrote a detailed explanation of why Earth must be at the center of the universe.

Not all early astronomers agreed with this theory, however. Aristarchus of Samos, a Greek astronomer who lived from about 310–230 BCE, thought Earth revolved around the Sun. But for two thousand years, Aristotle's geocentric theory was accepted by most scientists. The powerful Catholic Church, which relied on his teachings, also supported the geocentric idea because some biblical passages suggested that the Sun moved while Earth remained in one place. Few people were willing to dispute the church's favored theory. Anyone who challenged it was in danger of being imprisoned or even executed.

We have since learned that our planet is just a tiny speck circling an ordinary star, somewhere in a vast ocean of stars. Our understanding of the universe began to change around 1500, with the work of Polish astronomer Nicolaus Copernicus. Copernicus believed Earth and the other planets traveled in circular orbits around the Sun. His theory more accurately described the paths of the planets and stars in the sky than the geocentric theory did. But Copernicus's theory also removed Earth from its special place at the center of the universe.

Copernicus knew his idea was contrary to church teachings. Revealing it could be punished by death. He didn't publish his revolutionary idea until the very last days of his life. Copernicus's idea has been an essential part of cosmology ever since. The Copernican principle

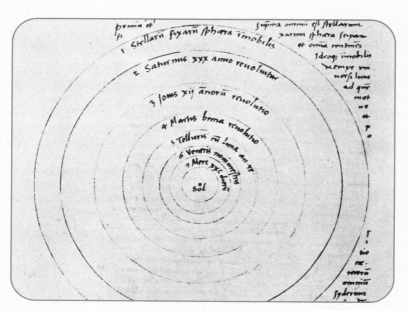

This drawing by Copernicus illustrates his idea that the planets revolve around the Sun (Sol).

says Earth does not occupy a special, central time or place in the universe.

In 1609 Austrian astronomer Johannes Kepler improved upon Copernicus's idea. Kepler used mathematics to analyze the orbits of the known planets and found that they all follow the same rules of motion. The planets, he discovered, travel around the Sun in elliptical (oval) orbits, not circles. Each moves more slowly as its orbit takes it farther from the Sun, then speeds up again as it moves closer. Kepler also found that a planet's speed is proportional to its distance from the Sun. The farther a planet is from the Sun, the more slowly it moves. In short, the motions of the heavenly bodies follow regular mathematical rules.

In 1610 the Italian scientist Galileo Galilei provided additional support for Copernicus's theory. The telescope had recently been invented, and Galileo made his own improvements on the instrument. With his new telescope, Galileo found four moons orbiting Jupiter. These moons were further proof that not every object in the sky circled Earth. Galileo's discovery made it easier to believe that planets could revolve around the Sun, much as the moons revolved around Jupiter.

Just as important, Galileo first explained the idea of inertia. Inertia is the property of all matter to remain in motion (or at rest) unless a force acts to change its motion. One such force is friction—the force that slows the motion of two surfaces that touch each other. Galileo realized that in empty space, without friction, an object like a star or a planet could keep moving forever. Through Galileo's work, astronomers came to understand that everything in the universe is in constant motion.

The key to understanding the motion of the stars and planets became available in 1687, when English physicist Isaac Newton published his laws of motion and the law of universal gravitation. Newton's laws predicted the motion of objects on Earth. Even more important, the same laws calculated the motion of the planets. According to Newton's laws, an apple falling to Earth and the Moon falling in its orbit *around* Earth both follow the same rules. Newton realized that the Moon constantly falls toward

Earth, but the Moon also moves forward fast enough to keep falling past Earth. That's how it maintains a constant orbit instead of colliding with Earth. The same laws of physics apply to the Sun, Earth, and the other planets. This may seem obvious to us. But in the 1600s, Newton's

THE MOON'S ORBIT

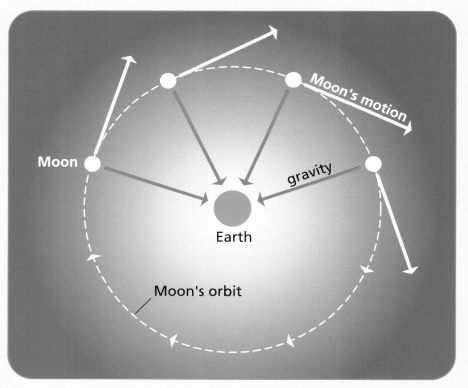

The moon is constantly falling toward Earth because of Earth's gravity. But the Moon's own motion is at right angles to Earth's gravity. This motion keeps the Moon in an orbit that follows the curve of Earth's surface.

laws were revolutionary. They allowed scientists to explain events happening far from our own world.

Astronomers continued to gather more information about the stars. Larger, more powerful telescopes let them see farther and farther into space. One of the objects that had puzzled early astronomers was the Milky Way. What was this faint streak of light painted across the night sky? Galileo was the first astronomer to see individual stars in the Milky Way. In 1750 English astronomer Thomas Wright proposed that the entire Milky Way was actually a broad band of many stars.

Astronomers were also finding small, fuzzy patches of light scattered across the sky. They called these objects *nebulae,* from the Latin word for "cloud." In 1755 the German philosopher Immanuel Kant suggested nebulae might be "island universes," or galaxies, made up of many individual stars. The word *galaxy* comes from the Greek word for "milk." The name we use for these large, spinning clouds of stars comes from the ancient name for our own galaxy.

The fuzzy "star" in the constellation Orion is the Orion Nebula.

British astronomer William Herschel studied nebulae through his telescope. He made a careful catalog of more than two thousand nebulae he found across the sky. Herschel confirmed Kant's hypothesis about the composition of these objects in 1785. His powerful telescope showed individual stars in several nebulae.

In the late 1700s, Herschel also studied the movement of binary stars—pairs of stars that orbit one another. He discovered that their orbits follow Newton's laws. This proved that Newton's laws were truly universal—they could be applied to objects anywhere in the universe.

ALL THE COLORS OF THE RAINBOW AND MORE

By the mid-1800s, astronomers were using photographic film to study the heavens. They kept their camera lenses open for long periods of time. This gathered much more faint light than you could with a simple snapshot. These long exposures displayed many thousands of stars invisible to the naked eye.

In the 1860s, English astronomer William Huggins was the first to study the heavens with a spectroscope. A spectroscope is an instrument that separates light into different wavelengths, forming a rainbowlike spectrum. Each chemical element gives off its own characteristic colors of light. So spectroscopes can analyze the chemical composition of stars trillions of miles away. Huggins found that the chemical makeup of distant stars was similar to that of our own sun. Astronomers have been analyzing starlight with spectroscopes ever since, instead of just cataloging the objects in the sky.

When viewed through a spectroscope, light from the

stars doesn't appear as a continuous rainbow of color. A star's spectrum also includes many thin black lines. That's because a star is surrounded by an atmosphere— a cloud of gas. Each element, such as hydrogen, in this cloud of gas absorbs certain wavelengths of light. Because these wavelengths can't pass through the star's atmosphere, they are not detected by spectroscopes. A series of black lines appears in the spectrum at these wavelengths. These lines tell astronomers which elements make up the gas surrounding the star.

Through early telescopes, all nebulae looked like cloudy smudges of light. But spectroscopes helped astronomers distinguish between two very different types of nebulae. Some are glowing clouds of interstellar dust and gas. Because their composition is different from that of stars, those dust clouds produce different wavelengths of light than stars produce. Other nebulae—ones that would later prove to be distant galaxies—shine with the characteristic spectrum of stars. They look "cloudy" only because they are too far away for us to see their individual stars. The two different kinds of nebulae appear very different when viewed through a spectroscope, because the light they produce is so different.

THE DOPPLER EFFECT

Picture yourself standing on the bank of a river that is flowing at a steady rate. Farther upstream a friend stands on a bridge, dropping Ping-Pong balls into the water at the rate of one per second. If you stand still, you'll see balls floating past you at that same rate—one per second.

Imagine walking upstream. The current carries the balls toward you as you walk toward the bridge. Because you're moving toward the source of the balls, you discover you are now passing more than one ball per second. The faster you walk, the more balls you will pass each second.

Now turn around and walk downstream. Since the current is carrying the balls in the same direction, you'll pass fewer than one ball per second. The faster you walk, the more the balls seem to spread apart.

In this thought experiment, your friend on the bridge represents a source of light—a star. The Ping-Pong balls represent light waves from that star. Like the balls floating along in the river, light moves through space at a constant speed. But if we move toward the source of the light, the waves (balls) seem closer together. And if we move away from the source, they appear to be farther apart. This is the Doppler effect. It's named for the Austrian physicist Christian Doppler, who first explained it in 1842.

Since sound also travels in waves, you've certainly *heard* the Doppler effect. As a sound moves toward or away from us, we hear it differently. Listen as a car drives past on the highway. As the car moves toward you, the hum of the tires and engine sound higher. As soon as the car passes you, the pitch of the sound becomes lower.

With light, we experience the Doppler effect as a change in color. Astronomers call it *redshift* or *blueshift.* In the spectrum, red light has longer wavelengths than blue light. When a light source (a star or galaxy) moves

The Doppler Effect

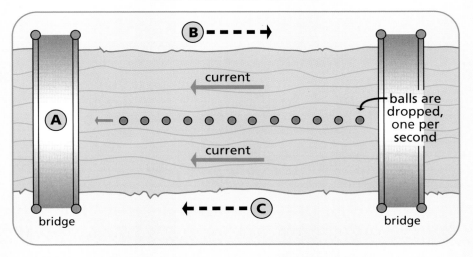

A. An observer who is standing still sees the balls float downstream at a rate of one per second.

B. An observer who is walking upstream, against the current, passes more than one ball per second.

C. An observer who is walking downstream, with the current, passes fewer than one ball per second.

away from us, its light waves are "stretched out," so the light appears redder than it would if the source were standing still. That is redshift. Blueshift occurs when a light source moves toward us. Its light waves are "compressed," so the light appears bluer than it would if the source were standing still.

Dark lines appear at predictable places in a star's spectrum. If these lines seem shifted toward the red end of the spectrum, compared to light from a stationary source on Earth, astronomers know that the star must be moving away from us. The farther the bands are shifted toward the red, the faster the star must be moving away.

In 1868 William Huggins found examples of both redshift and blueshift in starlight. This meant some stars must be moving away from us (redshift) while others are moving toward us (blueshift).

REDSHIFT AND BLUESHIFT

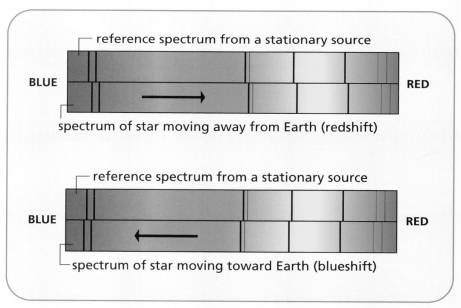

reference spectrum from a stationary source

BLUE   RED

spectrum of star moving away from Earth (redshift)

reference spectrum from a stationary source

BLUE   RED

spectrum of star moving toward Earth (blueshift)

A star's spectrum contains a series of dark lines. If a star is moving away from Earth, the lines are shifted toward the red end of the spectrum. If a star is moving toward Earth, the lines are shifted toward the blue end of the spectrum.

MEASURING THE COSMOS

How do we know how far away other stars and galaxies are? Astronomers use a series of different measurements that build on one another and can be used to check each other's accuracy. Together, these methods are known as the cosmological distance ladder. Here are some of the most important steps in that ladder.

Parallax: Parallax is the measure of the angle between two different views of an object. Hold a finger up at arm's length. Look at it first with one eye and then with the other. The finger appears to change position. That's parallax. The distance between your two eyes forms the base of a triangle. If you measure the angle separating the two different views, a simple calculation can tell you the length of your arm.

Astronomers measure the distance to planets and nearby stars by measuring visual angles and then doing simple calculations. To calculate the distance to a nearby star, astronomers use two angular measurements of the star taken six months apart, from opposite sides of Earth's orbit. The diameter of our orbit around the Sun forms the base of a triangle. Knowing that distance and the two angles, astronomers can calculate the distance to the star. Parallax can be used to accurately measure distances up to about 100 light-years.

Cepheid variables: Cepheid variables are large, young stars that expand and contract at regular intervals. Polaris, the North Star, is a Cepheid variable. In 1912 American astronomer Henrietta Leavitt discovered that these stars change brightness every few days or weeks in

Light-Years and Parsecs

Miles or kilometers are too small for measuring cosmic distances. Instead, astronomers use much larger units: light-years and parsecs. A light-year doesn't measure time. It measures distance. It represents the distance light can travel in a single year. Cosmologists use this measuring tool because the speed of light in empty space never changes.

A light-year is an enormous distance—almost 6 trillion miles (more than 9 trillion kilometers). But a light-year is still a tiny distance compared to the size of the universe. Proxima Centauri, the star nearest to the Sun, is about 4.3 light-years away. The nearest galaxy beyond the Milky Way, the Andromeda Galaxy, is more than 2 million light-years away. The most distant object we can see with our most powerful telescopes is more than 10 *billion* light-years away.

Astronomers also measure cosmic distances in even larger units called parsecs and megaparsecs. One parsec is the distance to an object that has a parallax shift of one second. (One second is 1/360 of 1 degree.) One parsec is about 3.26 light-years. A megaparsec is 1 million parsecs, or 3.26 million light-years.

a regular, repeating pattern. She found that the brighter the star, the longer this pulsing change takes.

Five years later, American astronomer Harlow Shapley used the pulse length to measure Cepheid variables' absolute magnitude—their actual brightness measured on a standard scale. Astronomers can also measure the apparent magnitude of a Cepheid variable in a distant galaxy—

its brightness as seen from Earth. Then they compare the star's absolute magnitude with its apparent magnitude. A simple calculation gives a good estimate of its distance. Observations of Cepheid variables can be used to measure the distance of galaxies up to 50 million light-years away.

The brightness of galaxies: Galaxies formed as gravity pulled huge clouds of gas and dust together. Early in a galaxy's history, many huge stars form. Those young stars burn quickly, with great brightness. Eventually they collapse and explode. Some of the gas from those explosions later forms new stars and planets.

Even with the most powerful telescopes, distant galaxies look like faint smudges of light. Light from these galaxies has taken a long time to reach us. So we are seeing light those galaxies produced at a much earlier time in the history of the universe. Astronomers can make rough distance estimates by measuring the brightness of these faint galaxies.

Galaxies are constantly spinning. The edges of a spinning galaxy move toward us and away from us at tremendous speeds. Because of the Doppler effect, the faster the galaxy is spinning, the more its light is shifted across the spectrum. By looking at the spectrum of a distant galaxy, astronomers can tell how fast it is spinning.

It turns out that faster-spinning galaxies are also brighter. So if you can measure how fast a galaxy is spinning, you can estimate its actual brightness. And if you know its actual brightness, you can estimate its distance from us. Astronomers use this method to estimate

STAR LIGHT, STAR BRIGHT   The closer you stand to a light source, the brighter it appears to be. Think about the headlights of an oncoming car. The closer it gets to you, the brighter the car's lights appear. The headlights aren't actually getting brighter. They simply look brighter as the car comes closer.

The same is true of stars. Some stars are actually much brighter than others. But some stars are also much farther away than others. A star may appear very bright in the sky simply because it is closer to us.

Astronomers talk about two different measures of brightness: apparent magnitude and absolute magnitude. Apparent magnitude is a measure of how bright a star appears to us from Earth. From our planet, Sirius is the brightest star in the night sky. Actually, Sirius is not much larger than the Sun. The cosmos is filled with billions of much larger stars. Sirius looks bright to us only because it is less than 10 light-years away.

Absolute magnitude is a measure of how much light a star actually produces, compared to other stars. Absolute magnitude doesn't depend on how bright a star looks to us on Earth.

distances of up to 10 billion light-years. This measurement is much less accurate, however, than those based on parallax or Cepheid variables.

Supernovae: A supernova is a titanic explosion of a star. A supernova can briefly outshine an entire galaxy. Several different types of supernovae exist. The kind of supernova most useful for measuring distances is known as a Type Ia supernova.

Type Ia supernovae occur in binary star systems (pairs of stars that revolve around each other) made up of a white dwarf star and a larger companion star. A white dwarf is the extremely dense remains of a star that has collapsed in on itself. It has as much mass as the Sun but takes up only as much space as Earth. The white dwarf's gravity gradually collects gas from its companion. When the white dwarf reaches a certain size—1.44 times the mass of the Sun—it collapses and explodes. Type Ia supernovae always explode at this size, so the explosions always have the same absolute magnitude. This brightness can be used to calculate distance. A supernova is vastly brighter than a single star. It can be seen at much greater distances—even in faraway galaxies. So supernovae can be used to measure the distance to those galaxies.

A Type II supernova occurs when a giant star runs out of fuel, collapses into itself, and explodes. Type II supernovae are even brighter than Type Ia. They can be seen at greater distances. But their brightness varies widely, so astronomers are less certain of distance estimates for Type II supernovae.

Because supernovae are so useful in measuring cosmic distances, there has been a great hunt for them in recent years. These rare events can be used to estimate distances of up to 10 billion light-years.

Chapter 2

Einstein Predicts an Expanding Universe

The German physicist Albert Einstein published his special theory of relativity in 1905. This theory showed that the speed of light is constant—186,000 miles per second (about 300,000 km per second). It's the universal speed limit. Nothing can travel faster. Einstein's theory also included the famous equation $E=mc^2$. In this equation, E stands for energy, m for mass, and c for the speed of light. In simple terms, it means energy and matter are just two different versions of the same thing. Matter is a form of "frozen energy."

In 1916 Einstein published his general theory of relativity. This theory gave us a new understanding of gravity and the shape of space and time. We usually think of space in three dimensions. But Einstein used a four-dimensional geometry created by the German mathematician Bernhard Riemann in the 1850s. Einstein showed that space is not an imaginary grid of straight lines. The shape of space is determined by the matter in it. Gravity is actually the warping, or bending, of space and time by massive objects. The greater the mass of an object—a star or galaxy, for example—the more the space around it curves. Smaller moving objects follow the curved shape of space as they fall toward or orbit around that object.

Einstein lectures to scientists in California in the 1930s.

Einstein's discovery was soon supported by experiments. In 1919 a team of scientists led by astronomer Arthur Eddington traveled to Principe Island, off the west coast of Africa. There they observed a solar eclipse. With most of the Sun's light blocked by the Moon, stars became visible during the day. The scientists measured the position of a distant star as its light passed very close to the darkened Sun. From nighttime observations, they knew the star's position relative to other stars in the sky. During the eclipse, the star appeared slightly out of place compared to other stars whose light wasn't passing as close to the Sun. The star's position was off by the precise amount predicted by Einstein's theory. The Sun's gravity had actually bent light from a distant star!

This artwork illustrates how gravity bends space. More massive objects, such as the black hole at bottom right, create larger distortions than less massive ones.

THE COSMOLOGICAL CONSTANT

In 1922 Russian mathematician Alexander Friedmann made a surprising prediction. Friedmann realized that the equations Einstein used to describe his theory of general relativity had several different solutions. But all of them indicated that the universe could not be static, or unchanging in size. Depending on the amount of mass it contained, it would either expand forever or expand and later contract. A Belgian astronomer, Georges Lemaitre, came to the same conclusion independently in 1927.

Friedmann's calculations raised the question: How

much mass is present in the universe? Is there enough mass to stop the universe from expanding and pull it back together again? Or will the universe go on expanding forever?

Friedmann sent his calculations to Einstein. At first ,Einstein thought the young Russian had made a mistake. Eventually, he rechecked the work and realized Friedmann was right. Einstein doubted this result of his own theory. At the time, there was no reason to think the universe was expanding or contracting. Like other scientists of his day, Einstein assumed the universe was unchanging in size. But if that were so, the gravitational pull of massive galaxies would eventually pull the universe together. To make his equations fit an unchanging universe, Einstein added a mathematical term to his calculations. It is the cosmological constant, represented by the Greek letter λ (lambda). In Einstein's equations, the cosmological constant counteracts gravity. It represents an imagined force that keeps gravity from pulling the stars and galaxies back toward one another.

By the late 1920s, evidence indicated that the universe is indeed expanding, as predicted by one solution to Einstein's original, unmodified equations. Because of this, Einstein later called the cosmological constant his "greatest blunder." More recent measurements, however, tell us it may not have been a blunder after all. It turns out there may be an invisible force causing the universe to expand. Cosmologists don't yet know what the force is, but they call it dark energy. Whatever it is, dark energy seems to have the same effect as Einstein's mathematical trick.

In 1932 Einstein and Dutch astronomer Willem de Sitter took another look at the shape of the universe. They calculated a third possibility. Instead of contracting or expanding, the universe could have a "flat" shape. In a flat universe, the cosmos would expand at first, but eventually gravity would slow the expansion almost to a stop.

ASTRONOMERS CONFIRM THE EXPANDING UNIVERSE

The first physical proof that the universe is expanding came from the giant 100-inch (250-centimeter) telescope at the Mount Wilson Observatory in California. In the 1920s, it was the world's most powerful astronomical instrument. Throughout that decade, astronomer Edwin Hubble photographed nebulae from Mount Wilson. In 1924 Hubble's photos proved that most nebulae were made up of billions of stars.

Hubble was able to find Cepheid variables in a number of these galaxies. Astronomers already knew how bright these stars are. Hubble used their brightness to calculate the distances of those galaxies from Earth. He estimated that the nearest, the Andromeda Galaxy, was almost 1 million light-years away. (The actual distance later proved to be more than 2 million light-years.) Hubble's discoveries showed that the universe extends far beyond our own galaxy. The universe includes vast numbers of other galaxies separated by enormous reaches of empty space.

Earlier in the 1920s, American astronomer Vesto Slipher had photographed dozens of nebulae. He discovered that the color of their light was shifted toward the red end of the spectrum. The amount of redshift meant each nebula must be moving away from Earth very rapidly. But Slipher didn't figure out what that meant. Before Hubble measured the distance to the Andromeda Galaxy, astronomers didn't know these heavenly objects were actually far beyond the Milky Way.

Hubble used a spectroscope attached to his telescope to examine galaxies in different parts of the sky, looking for redshift. In 1929 he reported that in almost every case, galaxies are moving away from us. What's more, the more distant galaxies are moving away faster than nearer ones. This turned out to be true no matter which direction Hubble pointed his telescope.

Hubble had discovered something amazing. The universe is flying apart at great speeds, in all directions. He expressed his discovery as what is called Hubble's law: the speed at which a galaxy is moving away from

Edwin Hubble *(center)* poses with colleagues Walter Adams *(left)* and James Jeans *(right)* outside Mount Wilson Observatory.

us depends on its distance. If Galaxy B is twice as far away as Galaxy A, then it is moving away twice as fast. This discovery gave birth to the Big Bang theory.

It's not easy to picture the idea of an expanding universe, but let's try. Imagine the universe as a rising lump of bread dough with a handful of raisins scattered through it. The dough represents space, and each individual raisin is a galaxy. Imagine yourself somewhere in the middle of the dough. Look out from one of those raisin galaxies at the neighboring raisins. (Ignore the edges. As far as we know, the universe has no edges.) All the other raisins—in all directions—are moving away from you as the dough grows larger and larger. This is true no matter which raisin you look from. In addition, more distant raisins are moving away from you faster, because there is more expanding dough between you and them.

Almost immediately scientists realized what Hubble's law meant. The universe must be expanding. It's not just that other galaxies are moving away from our own. Space itself is expanding, along with all the stars and galaxies in it. And if the cosmos is expanding as we move forward in time, then earlier in time it must have been much smaller. The farther back in time you go, the smaller it must have been.

Imagine a movie or a videotape of an explosion. When you play the movie forward, everything flies apart in all directions. If you play the tape in reverse, everything moves back toward the center. Eventually, everything is put back together again.

Another Way to Picture the Expanding Universe

If you have trouble picturing an infinite loaf of raisin bread, here's a two-dimensional model you can make to show the same idea. You'll need a large rubber band, scissors, red and black markers, and a metric ruler. Cut the rubber band to make a strip of rubber. Lay it flat on a table alongside the ruler.

With the red marker, make a dot in the middle of the rubber strip. That mark represents any galaxy—for example, our galaxy, the Milky Way. Now make a series of black dots, each 1 centimeter away from the next, on either side of the red dot. Your rubber band should look like this:

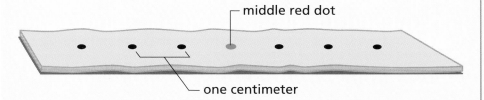

middle red dot

one centimeter

Next, hold the ends of the rubber band, and stretch it so it is twice as long. Notice the pair of black dots on either side of the red dot. They should each be 2 centimeters from the "Milky Way." Look at the next pair of dots on either side. They are 4 centimeters away from the red dot. The third pair of dots is 6 centimeters away.

The farther a black dot is from the red dot, the more it has moved away. Just remember, the universe has no center. Earth isn't located in a special place or time in the universe. As space expands like the rubber band, *all* galaxies are stretched apart. And the more distant they are, the faster they move away.

Do the same thing with a "videotape" of the universe. If you go back far enough in time, everything in the universe must have been in one place. The cosmos must have originated from a single point! That one point—whatever it was—must have blown apart, creating the universe and blasting it in all directions. Not just matter and energy, but even time and space were born in that moment.

The deeper astronomers look into space, the greater the redshift. The most distant galaxies are moving away from us fastest. The farthest objects astronomers can see with modern telescopes are called quasars (short for quasi-stellar radio sources). These are thought to be massive galaxies early in the process of forming. The most distant of these quasars are moving away at about 94 percent of the speed of light!

In the early 1930s, Georges Lemaitre suggested the universe exploded outward from a "primordial atom" or "egg." Lemaitre used Hubble's measurements to estimate how long ago the explosion had occurred. He calculated that the universe was about one billion years old. But that caused a problem. There were rocks on Earth older than that. Obviously, Earth couldn't be older than the rest of the universe. It turned out that Hubble's estimate of how fast the universe was expanding was too large. Later measurements showed the expansion is slower, and therefore the universe is much older.

The universe's rate of expansion is called the Hubble constant, or H_0. Astronomers have been trying to determine the constant's value since 1929. The current best estimate is about 14 miles (22 kilometers) per second per million light-years. A galaxy 10 million light-years away would be moving away from us at about 140 miles (220 km) per second. A galaxy 20 million light-years away will be receding at twice that speed—280 miles (440 km) per second.

AN ALTERNATE THEORY

Not everyone accepted the idea that the universe began with an explosion. In 1944 British astronomers Fred Hoyle, Thomas Gold, and Hermann Bondi proposed another idea—the steady state theory. They said the universe wasn't expanding as the result of a huge explosion. They thought the universe had existed forever, but small amounts of new matter and energy were being created throughout the universe all the time, resulting in the expansion Hubble had found. Not much matter would actually have to be created to make this idea possible—only about one hydrogen atom per year in each 35 cubic feet (1 cubic meter) of space. Until 1965 this possibility seemed as likely as an explosive origin of the universe.

Fred Hoyle was the man responsible for inventing the term *Big Bang.* In 1950 he used the phrase to poke fun at the theory he opposed. But soon everyone was using it. It was the perfect name for a theory that the universe originated in a single explosive instant.

Despite years of searching, astronomers found no evidence to support the steady state theory. And other new discoveries established the Big Bang theory as a better explanation for the expanding universe.

CHAPTER 3

Evidence Supporting the Big Bang Theory

The best evidence for the Big Bang is simply that the universe is expanding in all directions. Countless measurements confirm this. But many other observations also support the theory.

Three Degrees above Zero

You walk into the kitchen and find a warm pie cooling on the counter. By carefully analyzing the pie, you could find out a lot about how it was made. You might be able to figure out what ingredients were used and how they were put together. (This might require some tasting.) You could guess the temperature at which it was baked. And by taking the pie's current temperature, you could even estimate how long ago it came out of the oven.

That's a lot like the detective work cosmologists have been doing for the past fifty years. They study the universe as it is now. Then using the laws of physics, they try to figure out what it was like in earlier times.

In the 1940s, American physicists Ralph Alpher, George Gamow, and Robert Herman made one of the most important predictions based on the Big Bang theory. They started by picturing the universe as an expanding ball of gas. They knew all gases cool as they expand. So, they said, the universe must have been cooling ever since the Big Bang occurred.

You can experience this same cooling process at home. Release some air from an inflated bicycle tire. Inside the tire, the air molecules are the same temperature as the air outside the tire, but they are squeezed closely together under pressure. When you release the compressed air from the valve, you allow it to expand. As it expands, it cools. Even on a hot day, the air coming out of the tire feels cool.

The early universe was extremely dense and compressed. So it must have been tremendously hot. It's been expanding and cooling ever since. Alpher, Gamow, and Herman realized that even billions of years later, a little bit of that original heat would still be left. Because the universe has been cooling for billions of years, they calculated that the remaining energy would have a temperature of about 5°K—only 5 degrees above absolute zero. (Absolute zero, or zero degrees on the Kelvin temperature scale, is the coldest temperature possible. At 0°K molecules stop moving. Absolute zero is the same as $-459.67°F$, or $-273.15°C$.)

Alpher, Gamow, and Herman also knew the leftover heat would have special properties. It would take the form of blackbody radiation. Think of a blackbody as a closed black box in which heat has had time to equalize, so the temperature is the same everywhere. We can think of the entire universe as such a box—the biggest one possible. A blackbody gives off a characteristic spectrum of radiation. Because the energy of the Big Bang explosion would have been evenly distributed in all directions, the universe should have a blackbody spectrum.

ELECTROMAGNETIC RADIATION

Electromagnetic radiation is the movement of electric and magnetic energy from one place to another. It takes the form of waves that move at the speed of light. In fact, visible light is one form of electromagnetic radiation.

The distance from one peak of an electromagnetic wave to the next is its wavelength. The number of peaks that pass a given point per second is the wave's frequency. A wave's energy depends on its wavelength and frequency. Low-energy electromagnetic waves have a longer wavelength and a lower frequency than high-energy electromagnetic waves.

The different forms of electromagnetic radiation can be arranged according to energy to form the electromagnetic spectrum. From lowest energy (longest wavelength and lowest frequency) to highest energy (shortest wavelength and highest frequency), the categories of electromagnetic radiation are radio waves (including microwaves), infrared (heat) radiation, visible light, ultraviolet radiation, X-rays, and gamma rays.

If someone could find and measure the remaining heat from the formation of the universe, it would provide powerful proof that the Big Bang had actually happened.

But measuring the temperature of cold, deep space from our warm planet is not easy. No one managed to do it until 1965. Even then it happened by accident.

Arno Penzias and Robert Wilson were doing research on satellite communications at Bell Laboratories in New Jersey. They were searching for very weak radio waves coming from the Milky Way. Those waves could produce static in radio signals, causing communications problems.

Penzias and Wilson's instrument was a sensitive horn-shaped antenna. It was designed to capture microwaves. Microwaves are low-frequency electromagnetic waves. The waves they were searching for were very weak. Their

Robert Wilson *(left)* and Arno Penzias *(right)* stand in front of their horn-shaped antenna.

energy, as measured by their temperature, would be only a few degrees above absolute zero. The experimenters planned to measure the temperature by comparing their antenna readings of the Milky Way to readings of liquid helium, which has a temperature very near absolute zero.

Penzias and Wilson were careful experimenters. They spent a year checking every piece of equipment. Before they could measure the temperature of the Milky Way, their instruments had to read at or near 0°K when they pointed the antenna toward relatively empty space. Otherwise, they wouldn't be able to tell our galaxy's radio waves from other background signals the antenna might pick up.

But there was a problem. They couldn't get their instrument to read 0°K. No matter where in the sky they pointed the antenna, it kept reading 3.5°K. They tried everything, including cleaning pigeon droppings out of the antenna's horn. It still measured 3.5°K.

Finally, Penzias contacted Robert Dicke at nearby Princeton University. Dicke had invented the method they were using to look for weak radio signals. Dicke also had a team of researchers preparing to look for weak microwave radiation. But they knew exactly what they were looking for—the fossil heat from the Big Bang. Dicke's team expected the radiation to be spread evenly across the sky. And they had calculated it would measure about 3°K.

That was just what Penzias and Wilson had found. Right away Dicke knew Penzias and Wilson had beaten his team to the punch. He told them what they had actually discovered—the cosmic microwave background. It was the 14-billion-year-old remains of the Big Bang itself. Dicke's team later confirmed that the radiation fit the blackbody spectrum.

Finding the radiation Alpher, Gamow, and Herman had predicted was convincing evidence that the Big Bang had actually happened. For their work, Penzias and Wilson won the 1978 Nobel Prize in Physics. Their discovery has become one of the most famous experiments of twentieth-century science.

THE ELEMENTS THAT MAKE UP THE UNIVERSE

Where did all the elements that make up the matter in our universe come from? What do they tell us about the Big Bang?

In the earliest moments after the Big Bang, the universe was unimaginably hot and energetic. As the universe cooled, subatomic particles—particles that are smaller than atoms—began to form. Electrons came first. Then protons and neutrons formed, just one millionth of one second after the Big Bang.

Antiparticles also formed. Every kind of subatomic particle has a matching antiparticle. The antiparticle is a particle with the same mass but an opposite electrical charge. For example, the electron and the positron are antiparticles. So are the proton and the antiproton. When they meet, particle and antiparticle destroy each other in a burst of energy.

The particles whizzed around at tremendous speeds. They couldn't possibly come together to form atoms. Any particles that managed to combine were immediately blasted apart by other speeding particles.

As the universe expanded, it continued to cool. Within the first five minutes, some protons and neutrons had joined together to form atomic nuclei. But the universe would have to cool for about 200,000 years before those nuclei could capture electrons and become complete atoms.

What kinds of atomic nuclei formed in the early universe? George Gamow proposed that nuclei of all the elements formed within the first few minutes after the Big Bang. In 1948 he and Ralph Alpher described this idea.

The protons and neutrons of every atomic nucleus are held together with what is known as binding energy. Without binding energy, the positively charged protons in atomic nuclei would repel one another and the nuclei would fly apart. The larger the nucleus, the more protons it has and the more binding energy is needed to hold it together. Nuclear physicists soon realized that only the lightest elements could have formed in the Big Bang. The universe expanded and cooled too quickly to bind larger groups of protons and neutrons together to form the heavier elements.

Hydrogen is the simplest atom. It is made of one proton and one electron. Helium, the second simplest atom, has two protons, two neutrons, and two electrons. Scientists know how much binding energy is needed to produce each of the various atomic nuclei. They calculated that the Big Bang would have created a universe in which 73 percent of the matter would be hydrogen. Another 25 percent would be helium. Most of the rest

THE HEAVY
ELEMENTS
Hydrogen is the most common element in the universe by far. But stars and planets like ours have many heavier elements. For example, oxygen makes up almost 50 percent of Earth's crust, followed by iron (18 percent), silicon (14 percent), and magnesium (8 percent). Where did those elements—and even heavier ones like iron, gold, and uranium—come from?

Heavy elements are made in the cores of large stars. Stars turn hydrogen into helium by the process of nuclear fusion. In fusion, the nuclei of two small atoms join together to form one larger nucleus. The process releases large amounts of energy. When all of a large star's hydrogen has been fused into helium, the star begins to fuse helium into larger nuclei, creating all the elements up to iron. Finally, the star is out of usable fuel. It collapses and explodes as a supernova. The great temperatures and pressures of the collapsing star crush the star's atoms together. This creates nuclei of the elements heavier than iron. The exploding supernova then spreads these elements through the galaxy.

The Sun is a second-generation star. It was not among the first stars that formed after the Big Bang. The clouds of dust and gas that condensed to form our solar system were once part of other stars that exploded as supernovae billions of years ago. That's why our solar system contains elements heavier than beryllium. In a sense, our planet and our own bodies are made of stardust.

would be the simple elements lithium and beryllium. If measurements of the universe proved this prediction to be true, it would be more support for the Big Bang theory.

Each different chemical element gives off and absorbs certain wavelengths of light. When astronomers view the light from distant stars through a spectroscope, they can tell which elements they are seeing. These observations show matter in the universe is about 73 percent hydrogen and 25 percent helium. Lithium and beryllium make up most of the rest. Another prediction of the Big Bang theory has been verified.

EVIDENCE FROM PARTICLE ACCELERATORS

Cosmologists want to know what the universe was like in its earliest moments, long before planets, stars, or galaxies formed. They can't find out by looking through telescopes. Instead, they study nuclear particles too tiny to be seen by even the most powerful microscope.

A particle accelerator is a device that uses electromagnetic fields to speed up subatomic particles. Then it uses the speeding particles as bullets, smashing them into other particles or atoms. Experimenters then use very sensitive detectors to record what happens when the particles collide. American physicist Ernest O. Lawrence built the first particle accelerator, the Cyclotron, in 1931. Modern accelerators raise streams of particles to enormous speeds—more than 99 percent of the speed of light.

Particles in an accelerator have tremendous energy. They act much like matter in the very early universe. Studying these particles is like studying a tiny bit of the universe shortly after the Big Bang. Cosmologists examine the results of the collisions. Then they calculate how

matter and energy proba-
bly behaved in the first
moments of the universe.

THE AGES OF THE STARS

According to the best
current estimates, the
universe is about 13.8
billion years old. If as-
tronomers could find a
star older than that, we
would have to wonder if
the Big Bang actually
happened. On the other
hand, if all stars were
very much younger than

**The lines in this image are
tracks left by particles in a
particle accelerator.**

13.8 billion years, that too would cast doubt on the theory.

Astronomers estimate the age of stars based on their size.
Large stars burn brightly but use up their fuel in only a few
million years. The smallest stars—those about one-third the
size of the Sun—use fuel more slowly and can burn for billions of years. Astronomers estimate some of the small, dim
stars in our galaxy are about 11 billion years old. This is
within the age range set by the Big Bang theory. So the ages
of the stars do not rule out the possibility of the Big Bang.

INFLATION

Even after Penzias and Wilson found the cosmic background radiation in 1965, the Big Bang theory left many

questions unanswered. There was the "horizon problem," for example.

The cosmological principle is a central idea of the Big
Bang theory. This rule says the universe is homogenous and
isotropic at very large scales. *Homogenous* means that matter and energy are evenly distributed throughout space, like
a gas that is evenly distributed throughout a container.
Isotropic means that the universe looks the same from any
point of view. In a sense, the cosmological principle says the
universe acts like a gas—a gas made up of stars and galaxies.

From Earth we can see more than 10 billion light-years
in any direction. So we can see opposite regions of the universe that are more than 20 billion light-years apart. For the
universe to be homogenous, two such regions of the universe must have been able to equalize temperature. At some
time in the distant past, they must have exchanged energy.
(Think of a cup of hot coffee gradually cooling to room temperature by exchanging energy with the air in the room.)

But the universe is only 13.8 billion years old. In the
time since the Big Bang, the farthest energy could have
traveled is 13.8 billion light-years. Two regions of the
universe 20 billion light-years apart would never have
been able to equalize. Energy wouldn't have had time to
travel all that distance. This contradiction is known as
the horizon problem.

In 1979 a young nuclear physicist named Alan Guth
found a solution to this problem. In a flash of insight,
he realized that the early universe could have undergone a brief but tremendously fast period of inflation.
The universe had expanded *much* faster than the speed

of light. It turned out that a Russian scientist, Alexei Starobinsky, had earlier come up with a similar idea. Other cosmologists, including Andrei Linde, Andreas Albrecht, and Paul Steinhardt, soon developed and improved Guth's idea.

How could the universe expand faster than light? Einstein showed nothing can move faster than the speed of light. But inflation doesn't violate that law because it doesn't involve objects speeding through space. *Space itself* inflated at unimaginable speeds.

THE HORIZON PROBLEM

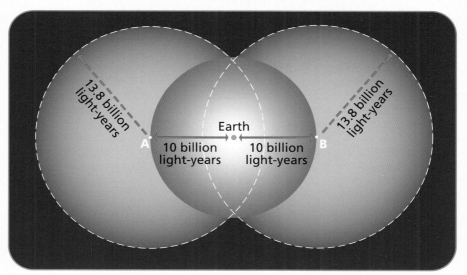

The idea that space itself inflated faster than the speed of light explains how regions A and B, which are 20 billion light-years apart, could have the same temperature even though energy has had time to travel only 13.8 billion light-years since the formation of the universe.

Guth described a universe that started out very small and developed huge amounts of energy and matter only as it inflated. No one yet knows what caused the universe to expand so rapidly for a tiny fraction of a second. But inflation filled the universe with energy, turning the first small bang into a very *big* bang.

Inflation solved the horizon problem. The very early universe would have been small enough to equalize its energy *before* it inflated.

Inflation also solved several other problems with early Big Bang theories. For example, inflation explains why the night sky is dark instead of being flooded with the light of billions of stars. Since the universe expanded faster than the speed of light, we can see only a tiny portion of it from our place in the cosmos. As a result, most of space appears black and empty. Light from the rest of the universe hasn't had time to reach us yet—and never will.

THE "LUMPY" UNIVERSE

An explosion in the middle of nothing should expand equally in all directions. If the Big Bang had been perfectly uniform, matter and energy would be spread out evenly. No part of the cosmos would have more gravitational pull than any other. So gravity would never have been able to pull matter together to form stars and galaxies. The cosmos would simply be a thin, cold gas.

When you look into the sky or even around your room, it's obvious that is not what happened. The matter in the universe isn't completely smooth in all directions. The cosmos is mostly empty space, but there are occasional clumps of matter—uncounted billions of galaxies, each containing billions of stars. There are planets and clouds of cosmic dust. So there must have been some unevenness in the original explosion to allow gravity to pull the stars and galaxies together.

Inflation solved that problem too. Quantum physics—the study of the behavior of nuclear particles—tells us there must have been small, random density differences in the infant universe. Those "quantum fluctuations" would have been magnified when the universe inflated. They would have become large enough to let gravity form the stars and galaxies later in the universe's history.

If that "lumpiness" can be measured, it should appear as slight variations in the cosmic background radiation. Those tiny differences would be strong evidence of inflation. But measuring those differences isn't easy. That's because any warm object produces microwave radiation. Earth itself gives off huge amounts of radiation. So does the atmosphere. If scientists could move their instruments away from the warm Earth, they might be able to measure the cosmic microwave background much more accurately.

In 1989 the National Aeronautics and Space Administration (NASA) launched a satellite called *COBE. COBE* stands for "Cosmic Background Explorer." The satellite scanned the sky for microwaves. It found the same background radiation that Penzias and Wilson had discovered. *COBE* measured its temperature more accurately—at 2.726°K. This measurement gave powerful new support to the Big Bang theory.

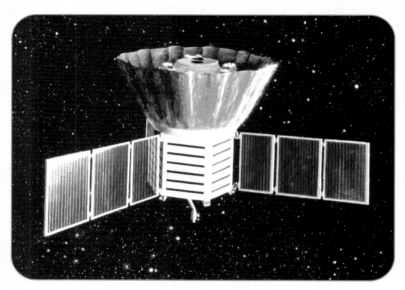

The *COBE* satellite

COBE measured and mapped this background radiation across the sky. It did find slight differences in temperature from place to place. The temperature differences were tiny—only about 17 millionths of one degree. But that was enough. Over billions of years, those small differences would allow matter to clump together, forming stars and galaxies. *COBE*'s findings told cosmologists that the early universe probably had undergone a brief period of inflation, as Guth had imagined.

Chapter 4

Open, Closed, and Flat Universes

Edwin Hubble proved that the universe is expanding. But what does that mean? For an answer, scientists turned to Albert Einstein's theory of relativity. Einstein's theory describes a universe of four dimensions, instead of the three (length, width, and height) we usually use. The fourth dimension is time. Einstein showed that the curvature of space and time is affected by the matter in it.

Using Einstein's equations, Georges Lemaitre, Alexander Friedmann, and Willem de Sitter calculated three possible shapes for the cosmos. The universe could be open, closed, or flat. Each shape predicts a different fate for the universe billions of years in the future. Since these possibilities are all four-dimensional and we are accustomed to thinking in only three dimensions, they are not easy to imagine.

In a closed universe, parallel lines eventually intersect. Cosmologists think of the shape of a closed universe as a four-dimensional sphere. Here's one way to picture this shape. Imagine yourself and a friend at the North Pole. You begin traveling south, side by side. You each travel in a straight line, following lines of longitude. As you go farther south, you move farther and farther apart. But after you pass the equator, you start getting closer again. Eventually you meet again at the South Pole. Now imagine that the North Pole represents the beginning of time—the Big Bang. Picture your travels as a journey through time. The globe represents the spherical shape of the universe. If you could somehow travel far enough in a closed universe, you might eventually (after a very long time) find yourself back where you started.

An open universe expands forever, at an ever-increasing rate. Think of the shape of an open universe as a four-dimensional saddle. In an open universe, parallel lines spread farther and farther apart. You and your friend start your travels at the beginning of time again. But this time, your paths diverge. The farther you go, the farther apart your paths spread.

The third possibility is a flat universe. In a flat universe, parallel lines remain parallel. Imagine again that you and your friend are traveling outward in time. This time, the universe expands like a sphere only at first. During this part of your trip, your paths move farther apart. But then the universe flattens out, and your paths become parallel lines. Time stretches on forever. Your paths never meet. They stretch out into infinity, side by side as parallel lines.

OPEN, CLOSED, AND FLAT UNIVERSES

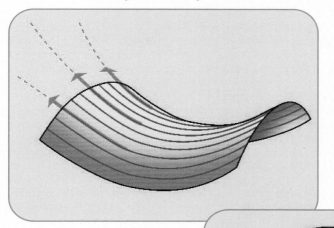

In an open universe, parallel lines spread farther and farther apart.

In a closed universe, parallel lines eventually intersect.

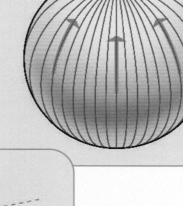

In a flat universe, parallel lines remain parallel.

So which is it? What is the shape of the universe? The most recent measurements suggest the universe is flat, but we still don't know enough to be certain.

RECENT DISCOVERIES

What is gravity's effect on the expansion of the universe? In 1998 two separate teams of scientists, one led by Australian Brian Schmidt and one by American Saul Perlmutter, tried to answer that question. They studied Type Ia supernovae in distant galaxies. These stellar explosions give us a rough measure of the distance to those galaxies. What they found was totally unexpected. According to their observations, the expansion of the universe seems to be speeding up!

In 2001 NASA launched the *Wilkinson Microwave Anisotropy Probe (WMAP)*. This satellite took an even closer look at the cosmic microwave background. *WMAP* was studying anisotropies—the same tiny variations in background radiation that *COBE* first found.

WMAP gathered more evidence for some form of inflation in the universe's earliest moments. It also gave us the best measurements thus far of the size, shape, and age of the universe. According to *WMAP*, the universe is about 13.8 billion years old and the rate of expansion of the universe—is about 14 miles (22 km) per second per million light-years. *WMAP*'s measurements seemed to show that the universe's geometry is flat but that it is expanding faster and faster. The data also indicated that the first stars formed about 200 million years after the Big Bang, much earlier than previously thought.

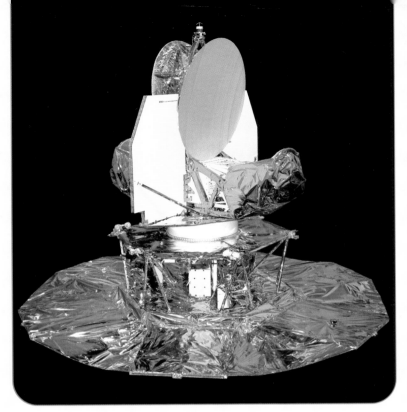

The *Wilkinson Microwave Anisotropy Probe* was launched in June 2001.

A SHORT HISTORY OF THE UNIVERSE

How did the universe evolve into the vast sea of stars and galaxies we see today? Here's how cosmologists think the universe developed. We'll start as far back in time as we can and take some snapshots of the expanding universe. Our first few snapshots will come tiny fractions of a second after the Big Bang itself. To measure these extremely short bits of time, we'll use scientific notation, or powers of ten. For example, the first snapshot will take place

10^{-43} seconds after the Big Bang. In ordinary notation, the number looks like this:

.000000000000000000000000000000000000000001

That's a decimal point followed by forty-two zeros and a 1—an unimaginably short instant of time.

The Big Bang: The universe arises from a singularity—a single point that is infinitely dense and infinitely hot. We have no way of knowing where the singularity came from or what happened at this moment. The laws of physics had not yet been established.

Snapshot 1: 10^{-43} seconds after the Big Bang, space and time are coming into existence. All the fundamental forces of nature—from gravity to electromagnetism—are combined into a single superforce. The entire universe is smaller than a proton. It is unimaginably dense and unimaginably hot—trillions and trillions of degrees.

Snapshot 2: 10^{-35} seconds after the Big Bang, gravity becomes a separate force. The other fundamental forces are still combined into what physicists call a "grand unified force." The energy of the early universe condenses to form massive, high-energy particles. For an instant, the universe inflates much faster than the speed of light. As the universe inflates, it also cools dramatically.

Snapshot 3: 10^{-32} seconds after the Big Bang, inflation ends. Virtual particles created in the vacuum (empty space) during inflation destroy one another, releasing radiation. This reheats the universe to trillions of degrees and fills it with energy.

The Four Fundamental Forces

Scientists believe matter is held together by four basic forces. These forces are—from weakest to strongest—gravity, the weak nuclear force, electromagnetism, and the strong nuclear force. Each force affects matter in its own way. Physicists learned much of what they know about these forces by smashing atoms together in particle accelerators.

Gravity holds us on Earth's surface. It holds the planets in orbit around the Sun and holds stars together to form galaxies. Gravity works over great distances. It seems strong, but it is extremely weak compared to the other three forces. It only seems strong when it affects large masses such as planets or stars.

The **weak nuclear force** controls some kinds of radioactivity. The weak nuclear force is at work when a neutron decays, breaking down to form a proton and an electron.

The **electromagnetic force** holds negatively charged electrons in orbit around each atom's positively charged nucleus. It also holds atoms together to form molecules. The electromagnetic force is the reason why vibrating electrons produce radiation, including light waves and radio waves.

The **strong nuclear force** holds quarks together. Quarks are the tiny particles that combine to form neutrons, protons, and other nuclear particles. The strong force also holds subatomic particles together in the nuclei of atoms. It is tremendously powerful at close distances. It has the strange property of becoming stronger as quarks are forced farther apart.

In the very earliest moments of the universe, the four forces were combined into one single force called a superforce. As the universe cooled and atomic particles formed, this one force separated into the four distinct forces.

Snapshot 4: 10^{-12} seconds after the Big Bang, the four forces known to modern physics—gravity, the strong nuclear force, the weak nuclear force, and electromagnetism—have separated from one another. Each now affects matter in its own way. The universe is full of high-energy particles blasted by powerful radiation.

Snapshot 5: 10^{-6} seconds after the Big Bang, the universe has cooled enough that quarks can combine into pairs and triplets to form neutrons, protons, and other nuclear particles. The universe is filled with speeding particles and antiparticles. A huge amount of high-energy radiation continues to smash into the particles.

It's important to remember that these first few snapshots of the Big Bang are speculation. They are scientific guesses based on what we know about how matter and energy behave. They are not yet supported by any direct evidence or measurements. However, beginning about one second after the Big Bang, the history of the universe becomes much more certain. There are many observations and experiments that support the Big Bang theory beyond this point.

Snapshot 6: One second after the Big Bang, most of the particles and antiparticles from the first moments of the Big Bang have destroyed one another, creating huge numbers of photons (particles of light). A small amount of matter is left over. This is the matter that makes up the modern universe.

Snapshot 7: Five minutes after the Big Bang, some protons and neutrons have joined together, forming helium nuclei and small numbers of lithium and beryllium nuclei. Most protons remain separate. They will later become hydrogen atoms. The universe is much too hot for complete atoms to form—high-energy photons knock electrons away from any nuclei that capture them. The universe continues to expand and cool.

Snapshot 8: About 200,000 years after the Big Bang, the universe has cooled enough for atomic nuclei to capture and hold electrons. Atoms form. Gravity begins pulling atoms together into clumps of matter. The first stars begin to form. The universe we know begins to take shape.

Free electrons absorb light. They also scatter (disperse) light, much as the droplets of water that make up fog scatter the beams of car headlights. Electrons in atoms are much less effective at absorbing and scattering light. So for the first time, the universe becomes transparent. Light can now travel great distances across the cosmos. Cosmologists call this photon decoupling. This is the farthest back in time we can see with telescopes. The light from that time is what we now measure as cosmic background radiation.

Snapshot 9: About 1 billion years after the Big Bang, the first galaxies form. The earliest stars collapse and explode as supernovae. These explosions create heavier elements and spread them through the galaxies.

Snapshot 10: About 9.3 billion years after the Big Bang, gravity has pulled gas and dust from the explosions of earlier supernovae back together to form new stars and planets. The solar system forms in the galaxy we know as the Milky Way.

Snapshot 11: About 13.8 billion years after the Big Bang, here you are, reading about the Big Bang. The visible universe is more than 27 billion light-years across. The entire universe is probably much larger.

CHAPTER 5

QUESTIONS YET TO BE ANSWERED

Thousands of experiments have supported the Big Bang theory. But difficult puzzles still remain to be solved. Here are just a few of them.

WHY IS THE UNIVERSE MADE OF MATTER?

When subatomic particles formed after the Big Bang, equal amounts of matter and antimatter should have formed. But everything we can see is made of matter. Astronomers find no evidence of leftover antimatter in other stars or galaxies. Why not?

Somehow, the Big Bang explosion must have produced an extra particle or two of matter for every billion particles of antimatter. After the particles of matter had annihilated all of the particles of antimatter, some matter remained. There was enough matter left over to form the entire visible universe. Why the universe formed in this way is still a mystery.

What Is "Dark Energy?"

Gravity should gradually pull the galaxies together and slow the expansion of the universe. Just a few years ago, cosmologists expected to see evidence that the expansion is slowing down. But their measurements showed just the opposite. The universe seems to be expanding faster and faster. What is causing this acceleration?

The energy powering the expansion is invisible to astronomers' measurements, so it is known as dark energy. We don't know what it is, but there must be an awful lot of it. Einstein proved that matter and energy are simply two different versions of the same thing. Dark energy accounts for about 73 percent of the universe's total mass/energy.

Dark energy acts as a kind of "antigravity." It pushes matter apart. Strangely enough, it acts very much like Einstein's cosmological constant, lambda. Einstein said that idea was his "greatest blunder." But maybe lambda wasn't such a blunder. Almost one century after Einstein included it in his equations, it turns out that there may be a force counteracting the force of gravity after all.

One candidate for dark energy is vacuum energy. Strange as it may seem, the laws of physics tell us that pairs of "virtual particles" can pop into existence from the nothingness of empty space. Each pair consists of a particle and its oppositely charged twin, such as an electron and a positron. The two particles quickly destroy one another, releasing a burst of energy. This vacuum energy may be at least some of the dark energy driving the expansion of the universe.

The spiral galaxy NGC 4603

What Is "Dark Matter"?

Each galaxy is made of billions of stars spinning around a central core. Galaxies are held together by gravity. Without enough gravity, individual stars would spin away into space and galaxies would soon fly apart. Groups of galaxies are also gathered together in great clusters scattered about the visible universe. Gravity holds these clusters together too.

In 1933 Swiss astronomer Fritz Zwicky studied the motion of clusters of galaxies. There didn't seem to be enough mass to hold them together. In fact, Zwicky found only 10 percent of the mass needed to produce enough gravity. There had to be more matter he could not see. Zwicky called the missing mass dark matter. In 1970 American astronomer Vera Rubin measured the spin of dozens of galaxies. Her data confirmed the missing mass.

Astronomers estimate only about 4.4 percent of the universe is ordinary matter. About 23 percent of the universe is composed of dark matter. (The rest is dark energy.) Dark matter is clearly more common than ordinary matter. But no one knows just what dark matter is or why we can't see it.

Some dark matter might be made of neutrinos. Neutrinos are tiny subatomic particles. They are produced by the trillions in the nuclear reactions that fuel the stars. Neutrinos are difficult to detect, because they don't interact with other matter. Millions of them are passing through your body as you read this, without affecting you in any way.

Scientists once thought neutrinos had no mass at all. But even if they do, they don't have nearly enough mass to account for all the missing matter of the universe. There must be something else—something massive but very difficult to detect. These mysterious particles, if they exist, don't interact with any scientific measuring devices. Physicists sometimes call these mystery particles cold dark matter or WIMPs (weakly interacting massive particles). Physicists have yet to detect even one single particle of dark matter, even though we can see evidence that lots of it must exist.

WHAT IS THE FATE OF THE UNIVERSE?

The universe is still expanding. Will it expand forever, or will it eventually slow to a stop? Will it then contract and squeeze back together again?

Cosmologists use the Greek letter Ω (omega) to represent the density of the universe. That is, omega compares the amount of mass and energy in the universe with its size. Whether the universe is closed, open, or flat depends on its density. If omega is greater than 1, the universe is closed. If it is less than 1, it is open. And if omega is exactly 1, the universe is flat.

If omega is greater than 1, gravity will gradually slow and stop the universe's expansion. Then gravity will begin pulling it back together. The universe will get hotter and hotter as it squeezes back together in a "Big Crunch."

After it contracts, would a closed universe "bounce"? Would it explode again, creating a new cosmos? Would that new universe follow the same laws as our own or completely different ones? There's no way to know.

There's another possibility. If there is not enough mass to stop it, the universe will continue expanding forever. Its matter and energy will spread apart farther and farther. The cosmos will continue to cool. After many billions of years, the temperature of everything in the universe will even out. The universe will be cold and inert.

So which will it be? A universe that squeezes back together in a Big Crunch or one that expands forever? At this moment, no one knows for sure. The most recent measurements show that the universe is still expanding faster and faster.

Until astronomers can accurately measure dark matter and dark energy, it will be hard to know how much gravity is pulling against the expanding universe. Only that will tell us what the ultimate fate of our universe will be.

Whichever it is, it will take many billions of years to happen. It will have no effect on our own brief lives. Nevertheless, it is still a fascinating question to consider.

What Exploded to Create the Big Bang?

The Big Bang was an enormous explosion. But what exploded, and what caused it to explode? This is a fascinating question, but it may be unanswerable. We have no way to gather information about any events before the Big Bang—if there were any. The explosion destroyed all evidence of anything that might have existed before it. Because time began with the Big Bang, there might not even have been a "before."

Quantum physics provides an intriguing idea, however. It tells us pairs of virtual particles can briefly pop into existence out of nothing. Could our universe have just appeared out of nothing in a similar way?

Is Our Universe One of Many?

Could other universes also have exploded out of nothingness? Some cosmologists think our universe may be just one of an infinite number of universes. They imagine endless "bubble universes" bursting into existence out of emptiness and branching off from one another in an eternal process of creation.

We may never be able to learn about other universes. Some cosmologists talk about the anthropic principle, which says we know about this particular universe only because it happens to have laws of physics that allowed for the creation of human life. No one could possibly know about any universe where humans could not exist, because no one would be around to know about it.

Some scientists suggest our universe may not extend an infinite distance in all directions. Instead, it could loop back on itself like a doughnut. If you set off in a spacecraft in one direction and kept going, you might eventually end up right back where you started. (This would still take a very, very long time.) Scientists are looking for repeating patterns in the cosmic microwave background that might confirm this.

It takes time for light to travel from the distant stars. So as we look deeper into space, we are looking back in time. When we view distant galaxies, we see light produced billions of years ago. Turn your eyes outward into space, in any direction. As strange as it may seem, no matter which direction you look, you are peering back in time toward the beginning of the universe.

Did the universe spontaneously erupt from nothing? Is it just one of countless others? We may never know. The cause of the Big Bang or proof of the existence of other universes may be beyond the reach of scientific experimentation. But such questions are not beyond the reach of the human mind. We can always look up at the stars and wonder.

Glossary

antiparticles: particles with the same mass but the opposite electrical charge, such as a proton and an antiproton

background radiation: the microwave radiation remaining from the Big Bang; also called cosmic background radiation

blackbody radiation: the characteristic spectrum of radiation given off by a body whose temperature has equalized

Cepheid variable: a large, young star that expands and contracts at regular intervals

closed universe: a universe that will eventually stop expanding and pull back together

cosmological constant (lambda): a term Einstein added to his general relativity equations to counteract the force of gravity

cosmology: the branch of science that studies the origin and structure of the universe

dark energy: the unexplained energy in empty space that is causing the expansion of the universe to speed up

dark matter: matter in the universe that cannot be seen but can be detected by its gravitational effects on other bodies

Doppler effect: a change in the frequency of waves from a given source when the source and the observer are moving toward or away from each other

electromagnetic force: the force that arises between particles with electric charge and binds atoms and molecules together

electron: a subatomic particle with a negative charge

flat universe: a universe whose expansion will eventually slow almost to a stop

galaxy: a very large group of stars, such as the Milky Way

general theory of relativity: theory that says that from a particular point of view, there is no difference between the effects produced by gravitation and acceleration

geocentric theory: a theory maintaining that Earth is the center of the universe

gravity: the force of attraction between objects with mass

light-year: the distance light travels in one year, about 6 trillion miles (9.5 trillion km)

microwave radiation: low-energy electromagnetic radiation

nebula: a cloud of gas or dust in interstellar space; also sometimes used to refer to a galaxy other than the Milky Way

neutron: a particle with no charge in the nucleus of an atom

nucleus (pl. nuclei): the center of an atom

open universe: a universe that will expand forever

parallax: the measure of the angle between two different views of an object

particle accelerator: a device that uses electromagnetic fields to speed up subatomic particles, then smash them into other particles or atoms

photon decoupling: event in the early universe when atoms first formed, enabling light to move freely through space

proton: a positively charged particle found in atomic nuclei

quantum physics: the study of the behavior of nuclear particles

redshift: the shifting of light toward the red end of the spectrum because the light source is moving away from the observer

special theory of relativity: theory that says the laws of physics are the same for observers moving at any speed, and the speed of light is constant for all observers

spectroscope: an instrument that separates light into its wavelengths

spectrum: an ordered arrangement of the frequencies of light given off by chemical elements in stars

strong nuclear force: the force that binds quarks together and holds protons and neutrons together to form atomic nuclei

subatomic particles: particles that are smaller than atoms

supernova: an exploding star

weak nuclear force: a short-range force responsible for certain nuclear reactions

TIMELINE

ca. 580–500 B.C.E   Greek philosopher Pythagoras teaches that Earth is spherical and rotates on its axis.

ca. 384–322 B.C.E   Aristotle writes that Earth is eternal and located at the center of the universe.

ca. 310–230 B.C.E   Aristarchus of Samos suggests that Earth revolves around the Sun.

ca. AD 140   Ptolemy writes detailed scientific arguments in support of the geocentric theory.

964   Abdurrahman al-Sufi, a Persian astronomer, first describes a galaxy outside our Milky Way in *The Book of Fixed Stars.*

1543   Copernicus writes that Earth and other planets circle the Sun.

1609   Johannes Kepler publishes his first two laws of planetary motion. He shows that planets revolve around the Sun in elliptical orbits.

1610   With his telescope, Galileo sees four moons orbiting Jupiter. This supports the idea that Earth is not at the center of the universe.

1687   Isaac Newton publishes laws of gravitation and motion, which demonstrate that all objects in the solar system follow the same laws.

1750   Thomas Wright suggests that the Milky Way is actually a collection of many stars.

1755 Immanuel Kant suggests that nebulae may be disks of many stars.

1781 French astronomer Charles Messier identifies more than one hundred nebulae, many of which will turn out to be far beyond the Milky Way.

1785 William Herschel concludes that nebulae are star clusters, as is the Milky Way.

1802 Herschel applies Newton's laws to the motion of stars beyond our solar system.

1842 Christian Doppler first describes the Doppler effect on light and sound waves.

1845 Dutch meteorologist Christoph Buys Ballot demonstrates the Doppler effect with sound waves.

1854 Bernhard Riemann creates a four-dimensional geometry that Einstein will later use to describe the shape of the universe.

1860s Astronomers use spectroscopes to distinguish between two types of nebulae—gas clouds and collections of stars.

1868 William Huggins demonstrates the Doppler effect on starlight.

1905 Einstein publishes his special theory of relativity, which shows that the speed of light is the universal speed limit and that matter and energy are equivalent.

1912 Henrietta Leavitt discovers that Cepheid variable stars have a definite brightness that can be measured by the speed of their pulsation.

1914 Vesto Slipher measures the spectra of fourteen spiral nebulae. He finds that most are shifted toward the red.

1916 Einstein publishes his general theory of relativity, which shows that gravity is not a force but the curvature of space/time.

1917 Harlow Shapley uses Cepheid variable stars to estimate interstellar distances.

1918 Shapley estimates that the Milky Way is about 100,000 light-years across.

1922 Alexander Friedmann uses Einstein's theories to describe a universe that must be either expanding or contracting.

1924 Using Cepheid variable stars, Edwin Hubble estimates the Andromeda galaxy is about 900,000 light-years away. (Later estimates will more than double that distance.)

1927 Georges Lemaitre proposes that the universe may have exploded from an "atom" or "cosmic egg."

1929 Hubble shows that galaxies are moving away from us. Hubble's law states that the more distant a galaxy is, the faster it is moving away.

1931 Georges Lemaitre first estimates the Hubble constant, the rate at which the universe is expanding. His estimate sets the age of the universe at about one billion years.

Ernest O. Lawrence builds the first particle accelerator, the Cyclotron.

1933 Fritz Zwicky realizes that galaxies and clusters of galaxies must be held together with dark matter.

1944 Fred Hoyle and others propose the steady state theory of the origin of the universe.

1948 Ralph Alpher, George Gamow, and Robert

Herman predict that remnant energy of the universe's formation should be detectable as radiation with a temperature of about 5°K.

1950 Fred Hoyle jokingly refers to the theory that the universe erupted in a single fiery explosion as the "Big Bang." The name sticks.

1965 Arno Penzias and Robert Wilson use their radio telescope to detect the remnant energy of the Big Bang. Their measurement of 3.5°K agrees with the prediction made by Alpher, Gamow, and Herman.

1970 Vera Rubin and others find evidence of dark matter in other galaxies.

1978 Penzias and Wilson win the Nobel Prize in Physics.

1979 Alan Guth proposes a period of rapid inflation in the very early universe.

1989 NASA's *COBE* satellite measures the cosmic microwave background at 2.726°K. It finds tiny variations in temperature that would allow for galaxy formation.

1990 NASA launches the *Hubble Space Telescope*.

1998 Teams of scientists led by Saul Perlmutter and Brian Schmidt find that the universe is expanding at an accelerating rate.

2001 NASA launches the *Wilkinson Microwave Anisotropy Probe* (*WMAP*).

2003 *WMAP* data indicate that the universe is flat, expanding, and about 13.8 billion years old.

Biographies

Albert Einstein (1879–1955) Einstein, one of the world's greatest scientists, was born in Germany. He was not a particularly outstanding student. After finishing his studies, he worked in the Swiss patent office. In 1905 he published his special theory of relativity and explained both Brownian motion (the random movements of tiny particles suspended in a liquid or gas) and the photoelectric effect (electricity caused by light shining on a metal). In 1916 he published his general theory of relativity. In 1921 Einstein won the Nobel Prize in Physics for his study of the photoelectric effect. Einstein, who was a Jew, fled to the United States after Adolf Hitler rose to power in Germany. He spent the rest of his life working at Princeton University. Einstein lived a simple life, working, sailing, and playing his violin. Meanwhile, the world revered him as a scientist, a supporter of the state of Israel, and an advocate for world peace and world government.

Alexander Friedmann (1888–1925) Friedmann was born in Saint Petersburg, Russia. He was trained as a mathematician and a meteorologist. He was adventurous and endlessly curious. He served in the air corps in 1914 and 1915, during World War I. After the Russian Revolution in 1917, he moved to the city of Perm, where he taught at Perm University. In 1920 he returned to Saint Petersburg, then called Petrograd, where he showed that the universe must be either expanding or contracting. Friedmann died at the age of thirty-seven, following an experimental balloon flight. After his death, the Soviet government honored his many scientific accomplishments by awarding him the Lenin Prize.

George Gamow (1904–1968) As a young student, Russian-born Gamow taught himself physics and calculus. His early career focused on nuclear physics and radioactive decay. He did research in Germany and Denmark before moving to the

United States in 1934. He taught at George Washington University in Washington, D. C., and at the University of Colorado. Gamow's research included work on the evolution of stars and the chemistry of the genetic code. He was known for his humor and his bold, lively personality. He wrote several popular science books, including *One, Two, Three . . . Infinity* and *Mr. Tompkins in Wonderland*, that explained difficult math and science in clear, understandable language.

ALAN GUTH (b. 1947) Guth was born in New Brunswick, New Jersey. He earned undergraduate and graduate degrees at the Massachusetts Institute of Technology (MIT). In 1979, while working at the Stanford Linear Accelerator in California, he proposed the idea of an inflationary universe. Guth later worked and taught at Columbia, Princeton, and Cornell Universities. He has spent most of his professional life as a professor of physics at MIT In 2001 he was awarded the Benjamin Franklin Medal in Physics.

WILLIAM HERSCHEL (1738–1822) Herschel, a German-born British astronomer, was the first to discover that distant nebulae are actually vast clusters of stars like our own Milky Way. Herschel built powerful telescopes that allowed him to see individual stars in several nebulae. He became famous for his discovery of the planet Uranus in 1781. As a reward, he was appointed royal astronomer to Britain's King George III. Throughout his career, Herschel's sister Caroline assisted him by carefully recording his observations. Herschel's idea that the universe is evolving is still a basic idea of cosmology. He also discovered the existence of infrared radiation.

FRED HOYLE (1915–2001) Hoyle was born in Bingley, Yorkshire, England. He was a British astronomer and mathematician known for disputing the Big Bang theory. He also gave the theory its name. Along with Thomas Gold and Hermann Bondi, Hoyle proposed an alternative theory—the steady state theory. During World War II (1939–1945), Hoyle helped create radar technology for the British navy. He also helped develop the idea that the heavier chemical elements are produced in the cores of stars. He suggested that life on Earth may have originated when comets "seeded" our planet with cells or spores from elsewhere in the universe. Hoyle was a multitalented man who also wrote popular science fiction novels. He was rewarded for his contributions to astronomy with a knighthood in 1972.

EDWIN HUBBLE (1889–1953) Hubble was born in Marshfield, Missouri. He went to college at the University of Chicago and then, as a Rhodes scholar, studied law at Oxford University in England. As a young man, Hubble was also a champion boxer. After practicing law briefly, he returned to the University of Chicago, where he earned his Ph.D. in astronomy. In the early 1920s, while working at the Mount Wilson Observatory in Southern California, Hubble began calculating distances to other galaxies. In 1929 he discovered that the farther away a galaxy is, the faster it is moving away. This discovery, known as Hubble's law, proved that the universe is expanding. To recognize Hubble's enormous contributions to astronomy and cosmology, NASA named the first orbiting space telescope in his honor.

GEORGES LEMAITRE (1894–1966) Belgian-born Lemaitre was a physicist and a Catholic priest. He spent most of his working life as professor of astrophysics at the University of Louvain in Belgium. He was an artillery officer in the Belgian army during World War I. After graduating from a Catholic seminary in 1923, he studied astronomy at Cambridge University in England. Lemaitre was the first to suggest that the universe had exploded from a "primeval atom" or "egg."

ARNO PENZIAS (b. 1933) Penzias was born in Munich, Germany. His family escaped from Nazi Germany to the United States in 1940. He attended City College and Columbia University in New York. In 1961 Penzias began work at Bell Laboratories in New Jersey. Robert Wilson soon joined him. In 1965 Penzias and Wilson made the first measurement of the cosmic background radiation—the remnant energy of the Big Bang. For their discovery, they shared the 1978 Nobel Prize in Physics. Penzias was a pioneer in the field of satellite telecommunication. Using radio astronomy, he investigated the chemical composition of interstellar gas clouds. He eventually became vice president of research at Bell Labs. He retired from the company in 1998. He is a member of the National Academy of Sciences.

WILLEM DE SITTER (1872–1934) Sitter was a Dutch astronomer and mathematician. He was born in Sneek, in the Netherlands. After studying mathematics at the State University of Groningen, he began work in the astronomy lab there. He later spent several years at the Cape Observatory in South Africa. For the rest of his life, Sitter was a professor of astronomy at the University of Leiden in the Netherlands. He studied the moons of Jupiter and applied Einstein's general theory of relativity to astronomical measurements. His writings introduced Einstein's new ideas to many other scientists.

ROBERT WILSON (b. 1936) Wilson was born in Houston, Texas. He attended Rice University and the California Institute of Technology. He began work at Bell Labs in 1963. With Arno Penzias, he found the remnant energy of the Big Bang. For their discovery, Penzias and Wilson shared the 1978 Nobel Prize in Physics. Wilson later became head of the Radio-Physics Department of Bell Telephone. He is a member of the National Academy of Sciences.

Selected Bibliography

Adams, Fred, and Greg Laughlin. *The Five Ages of the Universe: Inside the Physics of Eternity*. New York: Free Press, 1999.

Chown, Marcus. *Afterglow of Creation: From the Fireball to the Discovery of Cosmic Ripples*. Sausalito, CA: University Science Books, 1996.

Coles, Peter, and Francesco Lucchin. *Cosmology: The Origin and Evolution of Cosmic Structure*. 2nd ed. Chichester, England: John Wiley, 2002.

Ferris, Timothy. *The Whole Shebang: A State-of-the-Universe(s) Report*. New York: Simon & Schuster, 1997.

Fox, Karen C. *The Big Bang Theory: What It Is, Where It Came From, and Why It Works*. New York: Wiley, 2002.

Greene, Brian. *The Elegant Universe: Superstrings, Hidden Dimensions, and the Quest for the Ultimate Theory*. 1st ed. New York: W. W. Norton, 1999.

Guth, Alan H. *The Inflationary Universe: The Quest for a New Theory of Cosmic Origins*. Reading, MA: Addison-Wesley Publishing, 1997.

Kolb, Rocky. *Blind Watchers of the Sky: The People and Ideas That Shaped Our View of the Universe*. Reading, MA: Addison-Wesley, 1996.

Ryden, Barbara. *Introduction to Cosmology*. San Francisco: Addison-Wesley, 2003.

Silk, Joseph. *The Big Bang*. 3rd ed. New York: W. H. Freeman, 2001.

Further Reading

Fisher, David E. *The Origin and Evolution of Our Own Particular Universe*. New York: Atheneum, 1988.

Gallant, Roy A. *Earth's Place in Space*. New York: Benchmark Books, 2000.

Jespersen, James, and Jane Fitz-Randolph. *From Quarks to Quasars: A Tour of the Universe.* New York: Atheneum, 1987.

———. *Looking at the Invisible Universe.* New York: Atheneum, 1990.

Moore, Patrick. *The Universe for the Beginner.* New York: Cambridge University Press, 1992.

Rhatigan, Joe, and Rain Newcomb. *Out-of-This-World Astronomy: 50 Amazing Activities and Projects.* New York: Lark Books, 2003.

Websites

Build a Solar System
http://www.exploratorium.edu/ronh/solar_system/
Make a scale model of the solar system and find out just how big the galaxy is.

Mysteries of Deep Space
http://www.pbs.org/deepspace/
This website has an interactive timeline of the universe, information about the *Hubble Space Telescope*, and a trivia challenge.

Science & Nature: Space
http://www.bbc.co.uk/science/space/
This site covers a wide range of space topics including the origin of the universe.

Spacetime Wrinkles
http://archive.ncsa.uiuc.edu/Cyberia/NumRel/NumRelHome.html
This site has lots of information about Einstein's theories of relativity.

Wilkinson Microwave Anisotropy Probe
http://map.gsfc.nasa.gov/m_mm.html
This NASA website has information on the WMAP mission and the formation of the universe, plus an image gallery and a variety of animations.

INDEX

Milky Way, 13, 19, 29, 37, 38, 58

National Aeronautics and Space
  Administration (NASA), 47, 52
nebulae, 13, 14, 15, 28, 67;
  Orion, 13
neutrons, 39, 55, 56, 62, 67

parallax, 19, 20, 67
particle accelerators, 42–43, 55,
  67; Cyclotron, 42
particles; antiparticles, 39, 59, 68;
  nuclear, 55, 56; subatomic, 39,
  42, 55, 59, 62, 68; virtual, 64
Penzias, Arno, 75
physics; laws of, 64, 69; nuclear,
  44; quantum, 47, 64, 67
planets, 6, 8, 9, 12, 22, 42, 47, 58
positrons, 39, 60
protons, 39, 54, 55, 56, 67;
  antiprotons, 39

quarks, 55, 56
quasi-stellar radio sources
  (quasars), 32

radiation, 55; background,
  47–48, 52, 57, 65, 66;
  blackbody, 35–36, 66;
  electromagnetic, 36;
  microwave, 36, 37–38, 47, 52,
  65, 67
radio waves, 36, 37, 55
redshift, 16, 17, 18, 29, 32, 67
relativity: general theory of, 24,
  49, 66; special theory of, 24, 67

Sitter, William de, 28, 49, 75
space, 24, 30, 32, 65, 69
spectroscopes, 14, 15, 29, 69

spectrum, 68, 67; blackbody, 39;
  electromagnetic, 36
speed of light. *See* light: speed of
stars, 4, 5, 6, 8, 9, 16, 18, 22, 25,
  41, 42, 44, 47, 52, 58, 59, 61,
  65; ages of, 43; giant star, 23;
  Polaris (North Star), 20;
  Proxima Centauri, 19; Sirius,
  21; white dwarf, 23
Sun, 8, 9, 10–11, 12, 25
supernovae, 22–23, 41, 58, 68;
  Type Ia, 22, 23, 52; Type II, 23

telescopes, 11, 15, 19, 22, 29, 42,
  57

universe, 4, 5, 6, 7, 8, 9, 10, 14,
  20, 26, 27, 33, 42, 45–47;
  closed, 49–50, 51, 63, 66;
  density of, 63; expansion of, 7,
  60; flat, 49, 50, 51, 52, 63, 66;
  history (origins) of, 4, 6, 8, 54,
  56–58; open, 49, 50, 51, 63, 67;
  shape of, 28, 49–58; visible, 58,
  59, 61

wavelengths. *See* light
Wilson, Robert, 37–38, 39, 43,
  47, 75

Photo Acknowledgments

The images in this book are used with permission of: NASA, pp. 5, 61; © Bernd Koch/Peter Arnold, Inc., p. 10; Laura Westlund, pp. 12, 17, 18, 31, 45, 51; © Roger Ressmeyer/ CORBIS, p. 13; © Bettmann/CORBIS, p. 25; © Julian Baum/ Science Photo Library, p. 26; © AIP Emilio Segrè Visual Archives, p. 29; © Lucent Technologies' Bell Laboratories, courtesy AIP Emilio Segrè Visual Archives, Physics Today Collection, p. 37; © Fermilab/Science Photo Library, p. 43; © Markowitz Jeffrey/CORBIS SYGMA, p. 48; © NASA/Science Photo Library, p. 53.

Cover design by Tim Parlin.